How to cast your own
Spells &
Charms

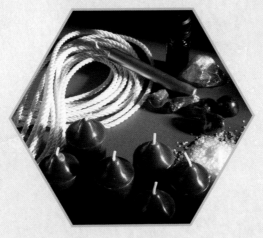

How to cast your own

Spells & Charms

SALLY MORNINGSTAR

LORENZ BOOKS

ABOUT THE AUTHOR

Sally Morningstar is a hedgewytch, a healer and creatrix of things magical. Her ancestral name originates from the Anglo Saxon for Magical Healer, revealing an ancient family connection with magic and healing. As a hedgewytch, Sally works very closely with the Natural World. She runs an online distance learning course in hedgewytchcraft and Natural Magic and also offers private consultations, spiritual mentoring and personal readings. For over 40 years, Sally has practised Eastern and Western mysticism, shamanism, tarot and witchcraft. She is also qualified in healing, photography and art. Sally makes ethical magical and spiritual items for sale through her shop www.theblissfulpixie.wix.com/emporium.

This edition published in 2015 by Lorenz Books, an imprint of Anness Publishing Limited
108 Great Russell Street, London WC1B 3NA
info@anness.com; www.annesspublishing.com
Twitter @Anness_Books

© 2015 Anness Publishing Limited

A CIP catalogue record for this book is available from the British Library

Publisher: Joanna Lorenz
Senior Editor: Joanne Rippin
Photographer: Don Last
Photographer's Assistant: Lucy Pettifer
Model: Louise Meddings
Illustrator: Anna Koska
Production Controller: Pirong Wang

Printed and bound in China

PUBLISHER'S NOTE

The reader should not regard the recommendations, ideas and techniques expressed and described in this book as substitutes for the advice of a qualified medical practitioner or other qualified professional. Any use to which the recommendations, ideas and techniques are put is at the reader's sole discretion and risk.

ACKNOWLEDGEMENTS

I would like to thank Steve Paine from the Pagan Federation for being so helpful, and Joanne Rippin, my editor, for her sensitivity. I give thanks to Mother Earth, to my father, and to all the spirit helpers for supporting each step I have taken on my magical journey. I would like to say a special thank you to the "Morning Star" for all the teachings she has revealed to me during my life. And in these times of change, I ask that we all learn how to listen to the Spirit of the kingdoms in our care.

THIS BOOK IS DEDICATED TO THE MAGICAL HEART THAT BEATS WITHIN US

PICTURE ACKNOWLEDGEMENTS

The publishers thank the following agencies for permission to use their images in the book. The Bridgeman Art Library: p18, Fitzwilliam Museum, University of Cambridge, UK, *Journey of the Sun god, detail from the inner coffin of Nespawershefi, Egyptian, Dynasty XXI* p40(r) Roy Miles Gallery, *An Angel*, John Strudwick. Bruce Coleman Ltd: pp8(br), 42(bl) and 49(l) Hans Reinhard, p22 Jens Rydell, p24(tr) Kim Taylor, p26(br). Peter McHoy: p42(br) Fine Art Photographic Library Ltd/Private Coll, p8 (br) *Midsummer Eve*, Edward Hughes ET Archive: p30(tr) *Saint Christopher*, Titian.

CONTENTS

INTRODUCTION

THE SPELLS

INTRODUCTION

The nature of magic and the universal mysteries have fascinated mankind for thousands of years. Archaeological finds dating back to Neanderthal man indicate that in these "primitive" cultures there was an awareness of our connection to everything that surrounds us, and of how we might influence elemental and spiritual forces.

Some scholars say that the word "witch" comes from the Old English word "witan" – to know – but it is more likely to have developed from the Old English verb "wiccian" – to cast a spell. Spellweaving, a very ancient art long associated with witchcraft, has been used for both good and ill. All things can be used to harm or to heal. When a spell is cast, it is the intention and concentration of the spellweaver that gives the spell its power, for either positive or negative results. The ethical spellweaver works only with good, or white, magic and takes a pledge to "harm none".

In this introductory book you will be guided into the correct main practices for spellweaving, so that you can feel safe and secure when casting any of the spells that are included. When practising natural magic it is important that you keep an open and humble heart; walking upon Mother Earth with gentleness will fill your life with many rewards.

Natural magic works positively with natural and elemental ingredients such as the planets and stars, gems and crystals, trees, plants, flowers, birds, animals and stones. This guide focuses on a natural magic that has evolved over many years from my own study and practice of shamanism, paganism and spirituality, and is a blending of these and other religious traditions from around the world. Spellweaving is not separate from God and spirituality, it is part of that consciousness. This book will show you how to develop a relationship with nature, so that you can weave your own unique natural magic, as you learn how to weave spells of beauty for healing, spiritual understanding, abundance and love, for you and for others.

A spell is very simple. It is a positive affirmation, using focused energy. Our universe has abundant energy which you can use for the good. In learning how to work positively with the elements, animals, trees, minerals, planets and stars, you can build your own magical bridge upon which you can walk quite safely, because all things are energetically connected. In weaving a spell, you shall receive. exactly what you ask for. I have no doubts that spellweaving will bring as much magic into your life as it has into mine.

LEFT: *Long revered by tribal people around the world and traditionally used as a smudging bowl, shells are particularly associated with fertility of both mind and body.*

OPPOSITE: *Natural magic works positively with natural and elemental ingredients such as crystals, gems and plants.*

SUCCESSFUL SPELLWEAVING

Before you begin to weave a particular spell in this book you should have put some care and thought into your preparation. An important aspect of successful spellweaving is effort; what you put in during these initial stages will set the energetic scene for the spell itself. Put concentrated positive energy into your quest for the correct ingredients. For example, if you don't add an ingredient because you cannot find it quickly enough, your spell will mirror that lack of effort and be rendered less effective. Treat your spells with love and respect at all times.

When spellweaving it is helpful to concentrate on yourself by performing ritual cleansing and by maximizing your powers of concentration. You also need to approach magic with faith, and with an open heart. Be realistic in what you ask for, riches, fame and issues of control are best left alone, otherwise you will move into the realms of dark magic, which is not the nature of this book.

WHERE TO SPELLWEAVE

Spells are traditionally cast outside, and for the kind of natural magic found in this book it will help if you can find a place of peace and beauty to work in. If you do not have access to an appropriate place, however, you can use a room in your house. If you have the space it should be a particular room or section of a room that is primarily dedicated to making magic. It is important to keep the atmosphere clean and balanced where you work. This can be done by cleansing it regularly with salt and burning purifying herbs (see the House Blessing Spell).

YOUR MAGICAL EQUIPMENT

Start to build up a store of general magical ingredients and equipment. The magic weaver will always need the following basic elements: natural sea salt, a length of white cord, frankincense and other incense, candles in various colours, crystals, special stones and gems of your choice, a selection of dried herbs, essential oils, gold and silver pens, silk and cotton fabrics and a variety of threads. You will also need some paper that is as natural as possible; this might be handmade paper, parchment, or simply unbleached plain paper.

LEFT: *Spells are traditionally woven in the open, in places of natural power and vibrant energy such as woods and forests, and by the side of lakes and rivers.*

RIGHT: *Those with an open heart, who believe in magic, have an ability to see fairies and angels.*

OPPOSITE: *The equipment and materials that are needed for weaving magic are easy to find, and can be used for many kinds of spells.*

PREPARATION

IT IS IMPORTANT TO GIVE YOUR SPELLS CAREFUL THOUGHT AND PREPARATION. YOUR EQUIPMENT SHOULD BE BLESSED AND THE INGREDIENTS YOU USE SHOULD BE CHOSEN WITH LOVE AND CARE. YOU MUST PREPARE YOURSELF WITH CLEANSING AND YOUR MIND MUST BE FOCUSED AND FULL OF ENERGY. YOU SHOULD ALSO HAVE TAKEN THE SPELLWEAVER'S PLEDGE THAT THE MAGIC YOU CREATE WILL BE FOR THE HIGHER GOOD.

ENERGETIC BREATHING

The most important ingredient in a successful spell is belief. The second most important ingredient is feeling. The more concentrated positive effort you fill your spell with, the more potent it will be. If you succeed in believing, 100 per cent, that your spell will work then it will. To build up your concentrated energy, you will need to learn energetic breathing. When you have mastered the technique, use it whenever you feel the need, particularly when you are weaving a difficult spell that you need all your powers for.

1 Make sure your feet are firmly set upon the ground, shoulder-width apart, and feel their contact with the ground. With your hands resting on your stomach, take a few deep breaths, deep in your stomach, to ground yourself.

2 Place both your hands just below the sternum. Begin to breathe, not too deeply, but slowly and with concentration.

3 On each inward breath, breathe through your nose, and draw golden light into yourself. Hold the breath for a short time and feel your heart opening. On each outward breath, breathe through your mouth, as you do so let the light circulate round your body.

4 Breathe this way until you feel energized and wide awake. Then rest your hands on the heart chakra for a few moments, breathing normally.

THE POWER OF HIGH MAGIC

BEFORE YOU BEGIN SENDING WISHES AND WEAVING SPELLS, BE WARNED! WHAT YOU GIVE OUT IN MAGIC RETURNS TO YOU THREEFOLD. THE ENERGY YOU PUT INTO YOUR SPELLS INCREASES AND GROWS AS IT IS RELEASED, SO BE CAREFUL WHAT YOU WISH FOR BECAUSE YOU MAY HAVE TO LIVE WITH THE CONSEQUENCES FOR A LONG TIME.

HOWEVER, BY ASKING WITH SINCERITY, YOU ASK FROM THE RIGHT PLACE, FROM THE HEART, AND THIS IS THE TRUE POWER THAT YOU HOLD WITHIN YOU. IT IS IMPORTANT NOT TO BE FEARFUL OF NATURAL MAGIC, BUT INSTEAD TO LEARN HOW TO BE HUMBLE AND HOW TO ASK FOR THINGS IN THE RIGHT WAY AND WITH THANKFULNESS IN YOUR HEART.

THE SPELLWEAVER'S PLEDGE

Before starting to weave spells of natural magic it is important that you pledge yourself to the light. This should be done simply and from the heart.

I Place your hands upon your heart and ask that you be filled with the light of love. Imagine the golden light and feelings of love filling your heart and then your whole being.

2 Let the light begin to radiate out in all directions around you, so that you are surrounded in an aura of its golden rays.

3 Open your arms and raise them above your head so that your palms are facing upwards towards the heavens and say the pledge. Then bring your arms down to your sides.

THE PLEDGE

I CALL UPON THE DIVINE WILL OF
THE UNIVERSE
TO SEND A BLESSING UPON MY
HEART, SO THAT
I MAY BE FILLED WITH
THE LIGHT OF LOVE AND TRUTH
IN ALL THAT I DO.
I PLEDGE THAT
FROM THIS DAY
I WILL DO MY BEST TO HARM
NONE WITH MY THOUGHTS,
WORDS OR DEEDS. I PLEDGE THAT
ANY MAGIC I PERFORM
WILL BE FOR THE HIGHEST
GOOD OF ALL.
SO MOTE IT BE!

Body Cleansing – Smudging

Preparation for spellweaving is traditionally done by bathing in water. Another form of body cleansing is smudging, or cleansing through smoke. The best herb for smudging is sage, but frankincense crystals or juniper aromatherapy oil can be used as alternatives.

1 Rub some dried sage into a ball in your hands and place in a heatproof bowl.

2 Light the ball of sage with matches and fan gently with a feather.

3 Using the feather, fan the smoke all around your body, including under your feet and armpits and the back of the body.

4 Pass the feather through the smoke when you have finished, to cleanse it.

Blessing and Consecrating your Equipment

All equipment that you intend to use for spellweaving should be cleansed and consecrated first. When blessed, the items can be stored carefully, ready for use. For the purposes of this blessing we will imagine a cord is being consecrated.

1 In a cleared space outside or on the floor, mark the four points of the compass. Moving clockwise, place an incense cone in the east, a candle in the south, a small bowl of spring water in the west and a small pile or bowl of salt in the north.

2 Light the incense. Turn to the east and say:

I CLEANSE, BLESS AND CONSECRATE THIS CORD
WITH THE POWERS OF AIR.

Then pass the cord through the smoke from the incense, while imagining a clear cool breeze passing through the cord.

3 Light the candle in the south, and say:

I CLEANSE, BLESS AND CONSECRATE THIS CORD
WITH THE POWERS OF FIRE.

Then pass the cord over the candle flame while imagining it being filled with warmth and light.

4 Turn to the west, where the bowl of water is placed, say:

I CLEANSE, BLESS AND CONSECRATE THIS CORD
WITH THE POWERS OF WATER.

Then dip the cord into the water or splash some water over it while visualizing a crystal clear waterfall cascading through it.

5 Turn to the north, where the salt is placed, and say:

I CLEANSE, BLESS AND CONSECRATE THIS CORD
WITH THE POWERS OF EARTH.

The flame of a candle can be used as a representation of the light and is a valuable symbol in spellweaving. Burning candles also represent the south wind – the wind of summer.

While sprinkling the cord with a pinch of salt and imagining stability and nourishment filling it with balance and harmony, say:

MAY THIS CORD NOW BE CLEANSED
AND PURIFIED FOR THE HIGHEST
GOOD OF ALL.

THE SEAL OF SOLOMON

THE SIX-POINTED STAR IS A MAGICAL HEXAGRAM, IT IS ALSO THE SYMBOL OF ANAHATA – THE HEART CHAKRA. IT IS THE INTERLOCKING OF AN UPWARD-FACING (MALE) AND DOWNWARD-FACING (FEMALE) TRIANGLE WHICH REPRESENTS THE UNIFICATION OF MALE AND FEMALE ENERGY. MOTHER MOON REPRESENTS RIPENESS, RHYTHM, REFLECTION AND UNDERSTANDING. SHE PERSONIFIES THE FEMALE ASPECT. FATHER SUN REPRESENTS GROWTH, EXPANSION, AND LIFE. HE PERSONIFIES THE MALE ASPECT.

THE SILVER CHALICE

To be a weaver of natural magic, you must work to better yourself and this can be done by developing the heart. To give, it is necessary to first learn how to receive in a truly open-hearted way. Use this visualization of a silver chalice to forge an open relationship between you and the Earth. This is a good exercise when you are focusing your energies for a spell but is also worth doing at other times.

1 Visualize that your heart contains a silver chalice if you are female, or a gold goblet if you are male, that is wondrous to behold. The chalice is decorated with precious stones, and apples and vines are embossed around the rim.

2 Imagine that golden light is falling down from the heavens through the top of your head and down into your chalice.

3 Allow the cup to overflow with sparkling golden light.

4 The light keeps falling from above as you let it overflow and cascade down through you to Earth, bathing her and you in golden light.

WORKING A SPELL

AFTER HAVING PREPARED YOURSELF, CONSECRATED YOUR EQUIPMENT AND GATHERED YOUR INGREDIENTS, YOU ARE NOW READY TO WEAVE A SPELL. EACH TIME YOU CAST A SPELL YOU WILL NEED TO CREATE A SPACE IN WHICH TO WORK, WHETHER INSIDE OR OUTSIDE. THIS SPACE SHOULD BE A SYMBOLIC CIRCLE AND MUST BE CAREFULLY CREATED AND CLOSED DOWN BEFORE AND AFTER THE SPELL.

MAKING A CORD CIRCLE

YOU WILL NEED around 9 m (29½ ft) of thin white cord (about 5 mm (¼ in) thick) to cast the traditional 2.7m (9ft) diameter circle, but it can be as large or as small as you wish. I usually cast my opening circle facing East – the direction of Air and Spring.

I Place the cord in an opened circle, with the opening in the east. Step through the opening with your ingredients and place them in the centre.

2 Close the circle behind you and seal it with a sprinkling of salt water.

LIGHT INVOCATION

BY THE POWERS OF HEAVEN AND EARTH, I CAST THIS CIRCLE IN THE NAME OF LOVE, LIGHT, WISDOM AND TRUTH, FOR THE HIGHEST GOOD.

3 Go "deosil" (clockwise) around the circle, sprinkling salt water on the cord. Visualize yourself surrounded in golden light. Hold your right arm out, follow your cord circle "deosil" with your finger and perform the light invocation. You are now ready to weave your chosen spell. Do not step out of your circle until your ceremony is completed.

Making an Offering

It is always advisable to remember your unseen helpers and to honour the spirit or energies of any equipment you use or place that you visit or work from. In making an offering to them, you are acknowledging them as important to you, this encourages their co-operation. Make an offering if you need special help, or in gratitude for a gift.

You will need 9 m (29½ ft) of thin white cord (about 5 mm (¼ in) thick) to make a cord circle (see opposite), plus a feather, a red candle, a bowl of water and salt.

1 Make a cord circle. Take the feather in your right hand. Hold it first to your heart then out to the east.

2 Say the dedication, "Hail to thee East (or other) Wind. I ask permission to work with your energies and call for your blessing upon this ceremony. I make this offering to you." Place the feather just inside your cord circle, in the east.

3 Place the candle in the south and light it, repeating the dedication, this time for the South Wind.

4 Continue with the offerings of water for the west and salt for the north, repeating the dedication each time. When you have finished, stand still for a few moments and then gather up your offerings and cord.

A Circle of Stones

You can make a magic circle using 12 stones instead of a cord. Purify and consecrate the stones by blessing them, placing a pinch of salt on each one, saying, "I bless this stone with love, light, wisdom and truth." Then sprinkle a circle of salt upon the stones, while asking for a blessing and dedication to light, to make a complete and consecrated circle around them. Touch each stone and welcome it to the circle, explain what you are going to do and ask permission to use it before you begin.

Closing a Spell

Closing a spell is done by walking or working "widdershins" (anticlockwise) until you end up where you started your spell. For example, if you worked your spell starting in the south, you close by beginning in the east and working back around your circle until you reach the south again.

1 Say: "I give thanks to all who have helped me and leave my request with you." Visualize the spell being taken up into the heavens by a spirit of light.

2 In a widdershins direction, gather up your ingredients, blow out any candles. Say "So mote it be" to ensure everything is closed and finished.

3 Make an opening in your circle and place all your ingredients outside the circle. Put all your organic ingredients onto the earth to be re-absorbed.

The Do's and Do not's of Spellweaving

Whatever you do, try to do it with gentleness and responsibility.

Seek no revenge and send no ill will – for whatever you send will return to you.

Remember it is illegal to pick wild flowers or disturb protected species.

When using herbs and flowers always work with petals or leaves in numbers of 3, 7 or 9.

If you feel you may have performed a spell wrongly, light a white candle and some frankincense. Burn the spell in the flame of the candle, saying "This spell is undone – so be it."

Do not manipulate the free will of another, or control events to suit yourself.

Always include the words "for the highest good of all" in a spell to insure against negative influence.

WHEEL OF THE FOUR WINDS

When making an offering to Spirit, or to the Energies, begin by facing east and work your way clockwise "deosil" around the circle from that point. The initial casting of a protective circle in this book always begins with the east, but your spell may call for another directional orientation. The four winds are also the four directions. Each wind has a different quality that rises and falls in its influence on the wheel of the year, as it turns. At the centre is the still point of the circle of life. Use this wheel to help you place your offerings or materials in the right position.

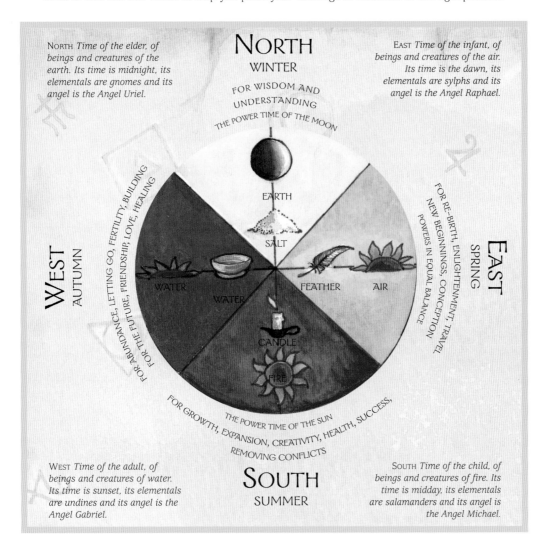

NORTH *Time of the elder, of beings and creatures of the earth. Its time is midnight, its elementals are gnomes and its angel is the Angel Uriel.*

EAST *Time of the infant, of beings and creatures of the air. Its time is the dawn, its elementals are sylphs and its angel is the Angel Raphael.*

NORTH
WINTER

FOR WISDOM AND UNDERSTANDING

THE POWER TIME OF THE MOON

EARTH

SALT

FOR RE-BIRTH, ENLIGHTENMENT, TRAVEL NEW BEGINNINGS, CONCEPTION POWERS IN EQUAL BALANCE

FOR ABUNDANCE, LETTING GO, FERTILITY, BUILDING FOR THE FUTURE, FRIENDSHIP, LOVE, HEALING

WATER

WATER

FEATHER

AIR

WEST
AUTUMN

EAST
SPRING

CANDLE

FIRE

THE POWER TIME OF THE SUN

FOR GROWTH, EXPANSION, CREATIVITY, HEALTH, SUCCESS, REMOVING CONFLICTS

WEST *Time of the adult, of beings and creatures of water. Its time is sunset, its elementals are undines and its angel is the Angel Gabriel.*

SOUTH *Time of the child, of beings and creatures of fire. Its time is midday, its elementals are salamanders and its angel is the Angel Michael.*

SOUTH
SUMMER

The Timing of Spells

TIMING IS VERY IMPORTANT WHEN WORKING WITH NATURAL MAGIC. IT IS ADVISABLE TO REFER TO A MOON ALMANAC OR LUNAR CALENDAR AND TO THE TABLES OF PLANETS AND DAYS OF THE WEEK IN THE SPELL TABLES, BEFORE YOU BEGIN A SPELL. YOU CAN THEN PLAN THE MOST SUITABLE TIME CAREFULLY.

Ancient civilizations such as the Babylonians, Syrians and Egyptians had great knowledge of the planets, seasons, spiritual energies and the power of herbs and minerals. When working with magic, it tends to be the phases of the moon that are most closely observed today, because the moon has such a strong daily influence upon the rhythms of ebb and flow in our lives. Moon times are shown in most diaries, or in *Old Moore's Almanac* (*The Old Farmer's Almanac* [US]).

The timing of spells is important because everything has a point or place of greatest power. By utilizing the correct face of the moon, or the four winds, the right planets, herbs, minerals and affirmations, you can increase their efficacy. There is a right time and purpose to everything.

It is important to leave your spell alone once it is cast. Do not keep repeating it as this shows a lack of faith in its original power. Spells can take time to materialize, so be patient. Don't think that your spell has not worked: it can take time to move things to where they need to be so that both you are ready and the circumstances are right for the spell's answer to appear in your life. Spells move in mysterious ways, so try not to be cynical if the results are not what you wanted – they will be exactly what your inner self called for to meet your true needs.

If you wish to utilize the powers of the moon more precisely when casting spells, refer to the lunar calendar which will take you deeper into working with the four faces of the moon as well as the stars. To remove an obstacle, for example, the best time of the year is the autumn and early winter, whenever the moon is in Capricorn, and during a waning moon. If you wish for love, the best time would be whenever the moon is in Taurus or Libra, and during her waxing moon face.

I have found that the moon and the sun have similar significance when travelling through the astrological signs; they are complementary sides to the same coin. The difference is that the moon tends to reflect to us what we need to learn or understand about

LEFT: *The God Ra was the Ancient Egyptian representation of the energies of the sun. Ra was venerated as the giver of light and life. The ancient worship of natural forces has been very instrumental in forming the natural magical practices that still survive today.*

that sign, while the sun manifests the sign's attributes in reality. For example, with the moon in a particular sign, you may think and feel things to do with that sign's attributes, and be shown your inner world in order to grow and understand. With the sun, you may find the attributes of a certain sign appearing in your outer world and circumstances, so that you inter-relate and expand your life in a physical way. The moon is potential, the sun is actual; the moon is inward, the sun is outward. When working with lunar magic, I burn pale blue or silver candles, with the sun I use orange and gold.

THE SACRED CIRCLE

To honour the spirit of nature and the cycle of the seasons, you will need to refer to the Sacred Circle of the Year, which shows the four main Celtic fire festivals. It also shows the four fixed solar points on the wheel, marked by the solstices and equinoxes. As well as these eight solar festivals there are the lunar festivals, called "esbats", which are celebrated on the first night of the full moon. Esbats are times of celebration and power.

For a lunar blessing on your magical equipment take up your equipment on the night of a full moon, and find a place outside where the moon's light shines brightly on the ground. Mark out a circle with salt, sprinkle jasmine oil – the aroma of the moon – upon the ground in the centre of the salt circle, then place your magical ingredients in the middle to ensure their protection during their time outdoors. Then, standing outside the circle, ask the moon for her blessing and psychic empowerment. Gather up your equipment, rub the salt circle away, and say thank you.

FOUR PHASES OF MOTHER MOON

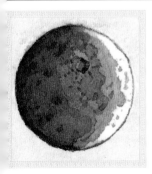

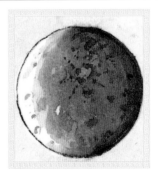

PHASE 1 WAXING
- east wind
- waxing moon (new)
- for new beginnings, conception, enlightenment
- to invoke – knowing

PHASE 2 FULL
- south wind
- full moon
- for increase and expansion, general fertility
- to expand – manifesting

PHASE 3 WANING
- west wind
- waning moon (old)
- to release something from your life
- to let go – courage

PHASE 4 NO MOON
- north wind
- no moon
- for wisdom, understanding, insight
- to learn – to keep silence

The Sacred Circle of the Year

Different regions of the world have different seasonal and directional patterns, but these important Celtic festivals of the year can be celebrated anywhere, following the seasons rather than these specific dates. Chart the seasons and directions that apply in your country of residence if they are different from below, but feel free to celebrate these festivals for Northern Europe, until you adapt the principles.

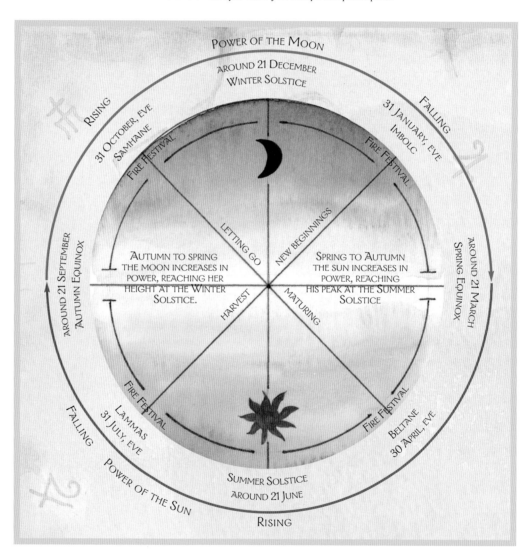

THE SPELLS

THE SPELLS THAT FOLLOW ARE SPELLS OF BEAUTY AND POWER.
APPROACH THEM WITH A HUMBLE AND OPEN HEART, PERFORM
THEM WITH ENERGY AND COMMITMENT, AND ACCEPT THEIR
WORKINGS WITH HUMILITY AND UNDERSTANDING.
DO NOT ATTEMPT TO HARNESS THE MAGIC FOR SELFISH
PURPOSES, OR TO BRING HARM TO OTHERS. IF YOU DO,
THE MAGIC WILL TURN AND WORK AGAINST YOU.
BE OF GOOD HEART AND YOU SHALL HOLD THE
KEY TO REAL MAGIC.
BLESSED BE.

MAGICAL WANDS

A WAND SHOULD REPRESENT YOUR ENERGY AND PERSONALITY AS MUCH AS POSSIBLE. FEEL FREE TO CARVE IT WITH SYMBOLS OR PICTURES THAT ARE IMPORTANT TO YOU. USE THE WAND TO CAST A SACRED CIRCLE, ENHANCE A SPELL'S POWER AND CALL UPON THE ENERGIES THAT THAT WAND REPRESENTS. THE MORE TIME AND LOVE YOU PUT INTO THE MAKING OF YOUR WAND THE MORE POWER IT WILL HAVE, SO CHOOSE THE DECORATION WITH CARE.

YOU WILL NEED

- 23 cm (9 in) willow stick (or a stick from another tree, see opposite)
- Knife
- Small, specially chosen crystal
- Sandpaper
- Copper wire
- Needle and thread
- PVA (white) glue
- Items appropriate to your wand's dedication:

  for general use add ribbons of the colours of the rainbow and top with a quartz crystal

  for love, two rose quartz crystals, dried roses, pairs of paper hearts and pink ribbons

  for fertility, seashells, river stones, sheaves (ears) of corn, green ribbons, and a pine cone

  for prosperity, coins, mint, almonds and horse chestnuts, and orange or gold ribbons

  for protection, rowan and oak , holly leaves and berries, rusty nails bound with red thread, red ribbons and flint

The willow is traditionally known as the wishing tree. She is also a tree of the moon. Tie a wish to her branches on the evening of a new moon if you want to acquire something, and during a waning moon if you wish to let something go from your life. Always explain what you are doing to the tree that you choose, and ask its permission and blessing first.

CUTTING YOUR WAND

1 Approach a willow tree with humility, and request that you can take a branch to make a magical wand. Cut it gently and say, "Thank you", leaving the small crystal as a gift.

2 While still standing with the tree and with the branch in your hand, ask for her blessing upon your magical wand by circling the tree clockwise three times, saying:

MOTHER WILLOW — TREE OF WISHES, BLESS THIS WAND WITH LIGHT. EARTH, AIR, FIRE AND WATER, BLESS WITH YOUR MAGIC BRIGHT. ANGELS OF THE HEAVENS, CIRCLE THIS AROUND, SPIRAL THROUGH THIS MAGIC WAND, TO GUIDE IT WELL AND RIGHT.

The Seven Sacred Trees of the Week

A wand of the right length should be both cut from its tree, and used in a spell, on the right day.

SATURDAY	ALDER	7.5 CM (3 IN)
SUNDAY	BIRCH	15 CM (6 IN)
MONDAY	WILLOW	23 CM (9 IN)
TUESDAY	HOLLY	13 CM (5 IN)
WEDNESDAY	ASH	20 CM (8 IN)
THURSDAY	OAK	10 CM (4 IN)
FRIDAY	APPLE	18 CM (7 IN)

Decorating Your Wand

1 Strip the bark away from the central wand and sand it down with coarse sandpaper. Sand it again with fine sandpaper until the wand is completely smooth.

2 Decorate the wand with appropriate items and ribbons. For general use, top the wand with a clear quartz crystal, binding it to the wand with copper wire, then glue bands of ribbons in the seven colours of the rainbow along its length. Use copper wire or a needle and thread to add anything else that feels right to you, such as a charm or tiny bells.

For a general wand, use these materials and add any personal item which you feel has particular significance or potency for you.

The colour pink and roses are associated with love; use these symbols to decorate your wand for a love spell.

These symbols of growth and fertility will give a fertility spell greater power. Larger items like these will need a sturdy wand. Use copper wire to attach them firmly.

LOVE SPELL

ASK FOR SOMEONE TO SHARE YOUR LOVE WITH BUT DO NOT NAME ANYONE,
OTHERWISE YOU WILL BE TRYING TO CONTROL HIS OR HER FREE WILL.
WHOEVER ANSWERS WILL BE RIGHT FOR YOUR NEEDS.

YOU WILL NEED

- Bottle of rose water
- 9 m (29¹/₂ ft) thin white cord
- 4 green candles
- Charcoal and heatproof burner
- Pink candle
- Rose petals
- Rose essential oil
- Cinnamon stick
- Gold pen
- Glass bowl, filled with spring water

ENVIRONMENT

 This spell is to be performed on a Friday, during a waxing (new) moon.

PREPARATION

 Cleanse yourself first by having a bath or shower then scent yourself with rose water.

1 Open your cord circle. Consecrate yourself by smudging. Instead of making different offerings to the four directions, light a green candle in each direction and invoke the winds:

HAIL TO THEE, EAST/ SOUTH/ WEST/
NORTH WIND. I CALL FOR LOVE AND
MAKE THIS OFFERING
OF LIGHT TO YOU.

2 Place some charcoal in a heatproof burner in the centre of the circle and light it. Light a pink candle next to it. Begin your energetic breathing until you feel emotionally charged.

3 You are calling for new beginnings, so face east. Put seven rose petals to one side then rub rose oil into the rest. Crush the cinnamon stick and place with the scented rose petals on the burning charcoal.

4 Focus your heart upon feeling love. Write the word "Love" in gold ink upon the seven petals you put to one side. Place them gently on the bowl of water.

5 Sit in the circle breathing in the scent of rose and cinnamon. Take time to centre and build up your charged energy. Open your hands, open your heart and speak your request seven times, with as much genuine feeling and emotion as possible:

O ANGEL ANAEL, I CALL UPON
YOU TO FILL ME WITH LOVE, THAT
I MAY FEEL A JOYOUS HEART. I ASK THAT I
MAY SHARE THIS LOVE WITH ANOTHER
WHO WILL COME TO ME OF HIS/HER FREE
WILL AND TOGETHER WE SHALL KNOW
THE BEAUTY OF A LOVING UNION.
I ASK THIS FOR THE HIGHEST
GOOD OF ALL.

6 Say "Thank you" at the end of the seventh request. Blow out the candles, close your spell and then your cord circle widdershins. Pour the rose petals and water respectfully upon the earth, or in a container of earth.

The dove is symbolic of Venus – planet of love and peace – and so dove feathers can be used when working a spell for love, romance or friendship.

SPELL TO REMOVE AN OBSTACLE

YOUR GIFT TO MOTHER EARTH, IN RETURN FOR HELPING YOU, CAN BE SOMETHING YOU HAVE MADE YOURSELF SUCH AS A CAKE OR A PIECE OF EMBROIDERY. IT CAN ALSO BE A LOVING ACTION SUCH AS PICKING UP LITTER, CLEARING A STREAM OR PLANTING A TREE.

YOU WILL NEED
- A gift for Mother Earth
- A fossil or blessed stone
- Natural sea salt

ENVIRONMENT
  Choose somewhere natural, safe and outdoors, where you feel comfortable and welcome. This spell is to be performed on a Saturday, on the fourth day after the first day of a full moon.

PREPARATION
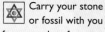 Carry your stone or fossil with you for seven days, from a Saturday to a Saturday. Talk to it, tell it your troubles, become its friend. Perform your spell on the seventh day, Saturday.

1 Take your gift and fossil to the place you have chosen to perform your spell. Beginning with the east, with the salt draw a deosil circle around yourself large enough to sit in, repeating the opening circle invocation.

2 Place yourself comfortably on the ground, facing north. Say the following invocation three times with as much feeling as possible:

MOTHER EARTH, I BRING YOU A GIFT OF (state what it is) BECAUSE I HAVE COME TO YOU TODAY TO ASK YOU TO HELP ME. I WISH TO REMOVE (state your obstacle). I ASK YOU WITH ALL MY HEART IF YOU WILL TALK WITH THE ANGEL CASSIEL ON MY BEHALF AND BOTH OF YOU HELP ME TO LIFT THE CONDITION BY HELPING ME TO UNDERSTAND WHY IT IS HERE, SO THAT I MAY MOVE FORWARD SAFE IN THE KNOWLEDGE THAT I AM PART OF A LOVING UNIVERSE.

TEACH ME, MOTHER EARTH, TO BE WISE AND TO TRUST IN THE BEAUTY OF ALL LIFE. SHOW ME THE WAY TO REMOVE THIS OBSTACLE SO THAT I MAY GROW IN UNDERSTANDING AND WISDOM.
(Take your fossil.)

I ASK THAT THIS FOSSIL, WHEN IT IS BURIED IN YOUR BEING, MAY TAKE AWAY MY BURDEN AND HELP ME TO ENDURE, BECAUSE IT IS WITHIN YOU AND YOU ARE WITH ME.

FOSSILS
Fossils link us to our ancestors and to earth's wisdom because of their long existence on the planet.

3 Say "Thank you" after the final round. Bury your fossil. Send the energies home by saying "So mote it be", while visualizing the completion of your task.

4 Leave the earth your gift, or tell her your pledge has been done (or will be done) on a certain date. With spellweaving it is important to give, or you may not receive.

5 Starting with the west, break your circle of salt widdershins and brush it away into the surrounding area, until you are back at west again. Walk away, leaving your troubles buried behind you. Do not look back.

The earth has an inherent ability to help us transmute our negative patterns and difficulties, rather like old vegetable peelings, which under her influence become high-quality compost.

PROSPERITY SPELL

IN ORDER FOR PROSPERITY TO COME TO YOU, YOU NEED FIRST TO GIVE SOMETHING OF YOURSELF FREELY, TRUSTING THAT YOU WILL BE REPAID. THE BLESSED SILVER COIN WILL MEAN THAT YOU GET AS MUCH HELP AS POSSIBLE WHEN YOU ARE READY TO WEAVE YOUR SPELL.

YOU WILL NEED

- Blessed silver coin
- 9 m (29½ ft) thin white cord
- Four large pinches of tobacco
- Gold candle
- 15 cm (6 in) square of orange silk
- Fresh spearmint leaves
- Orange thread

ENVIRONMENT

 Choose somewhere warm and private.

 This spell is to be performed on a Sunday, during a waxing (new) moon.

PREPARATION

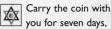 Carry the coin with you for seven days, from a Sunday to a Sunday. Perform your spellweaving on the seventh day, Sunday. Within the seven days, give something of yourself that costs time and energy without payment. Offer your gift to the Angel Michael. He will know that you are prepared to make an effort towards prosperity.

1 Open your circle. Begin with the east, making offerings of tobacco to each of the four directions. Stand in the centre of the four points marked with tobacco. Light your candle.

2 Take out your silver coin and hold it in the palm of your left hand. Hold the gold candle in the other hand. Repeat the invocation while facing south and passing your coin through the flame of the candle six times:

O ANGEL MICHAEL, I ASK YOU TO
HELP ME TO UNDERSTAND THE NATURE
OF ABUNDANCE, THAT I MAY
BECOME WEALTHY IN SPIRIT
AS WELL AS FINANCIALLY.
I ASK YOU TO BRING ME THE RICHES
THAT I NEED IN ORDER TO LIVE
COMFORTABLY. I ASK FOR THE RIGHT
AMOUNT OF PROSPERITY TO FILL MY LIFE
THAT WILL MEET MY NEEDS AND SO GIVE
ME THE TIME AND ENERGY TO USE MY
GIFTS, TO CELEBRATE LIFE
AND TO HELP OTHERS IN
POVERTY OR UNHAPPINESS.
GRANT ME THIS AND
I WILL REMEMBER TO GIVE AS
I HAVE RECEIVED.

3 Say "Thank you" after the sixth request. Place the coin in the orange silk square with some spearmint leaves and bind with orange thread. Carry this with you in your coin purse, or keep it in a container made of tin (the metal of Jupiter) in your home.

Tobacco is one of the sacred herbs of the Native Americans and is used in certain ceremonies to call in the energies. In magical terms, tobacco is sacred to Mars and is used in this spell to increase the strength and power of the wish.

4 Moving widdershins, gather up the four pinches of tobacco, saying "Thank you" to each of the four directions as you do so. When you have all four pinches in your hand, say "So mote it be" and visualize the spell being carried into the universe.

5 Place the tobacco underneath a tree, an almond or horse chestnut if possible, or an oak or field maple.

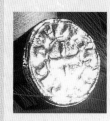

SILVER COIN

Take care of the coin, as losing it could indicate that you are forgetful or irresponsible with your money. If you do lose it, don't worry too much as it may mean that your finances will improve gradually rather than suddenly, or that money is not the answer at the moment. Replace the coin with one that you have passed through the flame of a gold candle six times. If this also gets lost, wait for 28 days before you attempt the spell again.

TRAVEL SPELL

FOR SAFE JOURNEYING, FIND AN UNUSUAL STONE AND MARK IT WITH THE ALCHEMICAL SYMBOL FOR AIR, WHICH IS THE WIND FOR TRAVELLERS. TAKE IT WITH YOU TO ENSURE YOUR OWN SAFE PASSAGE, OR GIVE IT TO SOMEONE ELSE TO CARRY UNTIL THEY RETURN.

YOU WILL NEED

- An unusual stone from your area
- 9 m (29½ ft) thin white cord
- Yellow candle, blessed
- Lavender incense or essential oil
- Aromatherapy burner (if necessary)
- Yellow and violet paints
- Artist's paintbrush

ENVIRONMENT

This spell is to be performed on a Wednesday.

PREPARATION

Find a stone that is different in some way from other stones in your area, perhaps in colour, shape or size. Take it home with you, asking permission of it first.

1 Open your cord circle and honour the four directions. Place the yellow candle and lavender incense or essential oil in the centre of the circle and light them.

2 Facing east, paint your stone yellow then draw a triangle in violet, with a line near its base, as shown. This is the alchemical symbol for air.

3 Hold the stone up to the east and as you do so, say the invocation eight times, making sure that you say "Thank you" after the eighth:

St Christopher is the patron saint of travellers. Medallions with his image are often given as gifts to loved ones who travel or move away.

O RAPHAEL, ANGEL OF THE EAST, FILL THIS STONE WITH YOUR BLESSING AND PROTECTION. I PRAY TO YOU FOR A SAFE JOURNEY FOR ME (or someone else's name). GUARD ME (or other) AND GUIDE ME (or other) ON THE PATH THIS JOURNEY TAKES, UNTIL I (or other) CAN RETURN.

4 Close your spell and circle in the usual way. Carry your stone with you on your journey.

SPELL TO IMPROVE YOUR BUSINESS

REPEAT THIS SPELL REGULARLY TO KEEP YOUR BUSINESS AFFAIRS FLOWING SMOOTHLY.
GIVING A GIFT TO THE ENERGIES THAT ARE HELPING YOU WITH YOUR BUSINESS PLEASES THEM
AND ENCOURAGES THEM TO WORK POSITIVELY ON YOUR BEHALF.

YOU WILL NEED

- 3, 7 or 9 fresh
  basil leaves
- Bowl of spring water
- Citrine
- Dried ears of corn
- Rice grains
- Mint leaves

ENVIRONMENT

This spell can be performed once a month on the first day of a new moon.

1 Bless your equipment and ingredients. Soak the basil leaves in the bowl of water for about 1 hour, stirring occasionally in a deosil direction.

2 Beginning to the right of the entrance, walk deosil around your building or work area, sprinkling the aromatic water as you go and repeating the invocation:

BUSINESS EXPAND, BUSINESS GROW,
SECURE AND SUCCESSFUL —
MY DEALINGS FLOW.

3 Rice and corn symbolize new life and will encourage fertile opportunities in your business. Bless the citrine, corn, rice and mint leaves, then place the citrine where you keep your money or transactions. Offer the corn and the rice to the energies that are helping you with your business generally, by sprinkling them in discreet places around your office or workplace.

4 Carry the mint leaves in your money pocket. Replace them with fresh ones each time you re-work the spell.

PSYCHIC PROTECTION SPELL

THESE SPELLS WILL SAFELY REMOVE ANY NEGATIVE VIBRATIONS FROM YOUR HOME OR FROM YOURSELF BY BURYING THEM IN THE EARTH. BE CAREFUL NOT TO INADVERTENTLY SEND OUT ANY ILL WILL IN RETURN.

YOU WILL NEED

- Pieces of flint
- Onions (1 for each room in your house)
- Red thread
- Red fabric
- Garlic clove
- Rosemary sprigs
- Red candle
- Frankincense
- Carnelian stone
- Vervain

ENVIRONMENT

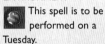 This spell is to be performed on a Tuesday.

SPELL FOR YOUR HOME

1 Place the pieces of flint in the centre of the area of your home you feel most uncomfortable in. Ask the flints the following:

PLEASE BECOME MY HELPERS IN REMOVING ANY NEGATIVE PSYCHIC ENERGY FROM MY ENVIRONMENT. I ASK THAT YOU BECOME THE FOCUS OF ANY NEGATIVITY TOWARDS THIS PLACE AND THANK YOU, GRANDFATHER AND GRANDMOTHER STONES, FOR HELPING ME.

2 Leave the flints alone while you continue with the next stage. Peel one onion for each room. Suspend each one on a red thread and hang them at windows in various parts of your home, repeating the following:

I ASK THAT THIS ONION ABSORB ALL NEGATIVE VIBRATIONS THAT ARE ENTERING THIS PLACE. THANK YOU.

3 Leave the onions in place for seven days, then gather them up into the red fabric with a clove of garlic, making sure that you do not touch them with your bare skin. Tie the fabric with a red thread and take it outside the boundaries of your home, preferably at a crossroads. Bury it, saying:

MOTHER, I BRING YOU THESE FOR YOUR CLEANSING TOUCH.

4 Collect your pieces of flint and place one either side and outside the doorways to your property. Place the others in the corners of the boundary to your garden or land, re-affirming your request that they remain the absorbers of any negative psychic activity.

5 Place rosemary sprigs on all the windowsills, then light the red candle and frankincense. As they burn, visualize your home surrounded in a globe of golden light, with blue flames around the outside. Call for:

PEACE IN ALL UNIVERSES — MAY ALL WHO WISH HARM BE HEALED OF THEIR IGNORANCE.

6 Do not use this candle again. Once the spell is completed, bury it as you did the onions.

Vervain is used in magic to protect, enhance and purify. Anointing your magical equipment with vervain will ensure that you and they are kept clean and protected.

PROTECTION FOR YOURSELF

Visualize yourself enclosed in a golden globe of pale blue light, with orange flames around the circumference. Repeat this powerful invocation once only:

RING PASS NOT

OR Cross your arms, legs and as many fingers and toes as you can, whenever you feel under attack. Visualize yourself in a ball of violet light. Imagine that you are inside a circular mirror, with the glass pointing outwards. Visualize that all negativity is now being reflected back to the sender. Keep your own feelings separate and send no ill will in return.

OR Carry a blessed carnelian stone anointed with vervain flower essence or a sprig of the vervain herb itself, wrapped in a piece of red cloth that is tied with red thread.

CARNELIAN STONE

Carnelian has the ability to protect you from negativity and helps to stabilize unbalanced energy in your surroundings. The stone is connected to hara, the personal power centre or Shaman's Cave, and so links you to your own inner power and strength during times of extreme psychic stress.

SPELL FOR GOOD HEALTH

EACH PLANET HAS ITS OWN MAGIC SQUARE WHICH CAN BE USED TO HARNESS ITS POWERS. THE MAGIC SQUARE OF THE SUN IS USED IN THIS SPELL FOR HEALTH, IT CAN ALSO BE USED FOR SUCCESS AND PROSPERITY.

YOU WILL NEED
- 9 m (29½ ft) thin white cord
- Gold candle
- Frankincense
- Gold pen
- 15 cm (6 in) square of natural paper
- Ruler

ENVIRONMENT
 This spell is to be performed on a Sunday during a waxing (new) or full moon.

1 Open your circle taking with you all the ingredients for the spell. Put the gold candle and frankincense in the centre and light them. Sitting facing south inside the circle, translate your first name into numbers by using the numbers below. For example, the name Mary becomes 4197.

1	2	3	4	5	6	7	8	9
A	B	C	D	E	F	G	H	I
J	K	L	M	N	O	P	Q	R
S	T	U	V	W	X	Y	Z	

2 Use the Magic Square of the Sun to work out the sigil of your name by drawing a line through the appropriate numbers so that it forms a pattern. For example, Mary – 4197 – becomes the sigil shown opposite.

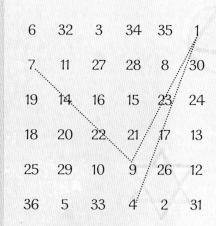

6	32	3	34	35	1
7	11	27	28	8	30
19	14	16	15	23	24
18	20	22	21	17	13
25	29	10	9	26	12
36	5	33	4	2	31

THE MAGIC SQUARE OF THE SUN
Use the square to mark out the sigil of your name. The sigil for Mary has been added here. Use the Magic Square of the Sun for invocations for health, wealth and success.

3 Using the gold pen, mark a 7.5 cm (3 in) square in the top right-hand corner of the paper. Draw your sigil in this square. On the back of the piece of paper copy the sigil of the sun and the words "Angel Och".

This is the sigil of the sun, copy it onto your piece of paper to increase the power of the spell.

4 Hold the piece of paper to your heart, with your sigil facing inwards, and visualize golden orange light filling your heart and then the whole of your body. Repeat:

I AM HEALTHY AND WELL.

5 Then take a strand of your hair and lay it on the spell. Fold the piece of paper six times so that it forms a small packet. Keep it in a very safe place, or preferably carry it with you near to your heart.

FEMALE FERTILITY GARLAND

IT IS VERY IMPORTANT THAT THIS SPELL IS PERFORMED ON THE FIRST DAY OF THE FULL MOON. WEAVE A CIRCLE OF HAZEL TWIGS TO MAKE A GARLAND THEN INVOKE DIANA, THE GODDESS OF FERTILITY, AS YOU DECORATE IT WITH NUTS AND PINE CONES GATHERED IN THE WOODS OR FOREST.

YOU WILL NEED
- 9 m (29½ ft) thin white cord
- Aromatherapy burner
- Jasmine oil
- Green candle
- Hazel twigs
- Green thread
- Acorns, walnuts, hazelnuts and/or pine cones
- Cinnamon sticks
- Green ribbon
- Rice wine (optional)

ENVIRONMENT
 This spell is to be performed on a Monday after your menstruation is completely finished, and on the first day of a full moon.

1 Bless, consecrate and open your cord circle. Place the aromatherapy burner filled with nine drops of jasmine oil in the centre, saying as you light it:

HAIL TO YOU, LEVANAH. I HONOUR YOUR PRESENCE WITH THIS AROMA AND ASK YOU TO HELP ME WITH MY REQUEST.

Light the green candle, while saying:
HAIL TO THEE, NOGAH. I HONOUR YOU WITH THIS FLAME OF LIGHT AND ASK YOU TO HELP ME WITH MY REQUEST.

Point your right hand to the heavens and say:
FATHER OF THE SKIES, I ASK FOR THE FERTILE SEED OF LIFE TO ENTER ME.

Touch the earth with your left hand and say:
MOTHER OF THE EARTH, I ASK FOR THE EGG OF LIFE TO BE MADE FERTILE.

2 Sit down on the ground, facing south. Weave the hazel twigs together to make a circle and bind them with green thread.

3 Take the nuts and cones and pour out nine drops of jasmine oil. Anoint each nut or cone with oil, saying the following invocation with intense feeling:

Nuts and pine cones and rice have long been associated with fertility spells. Cinnamon, a potent spice of the sun, is used to represent male energy and to increase the passion and vigour of this spell.

O DIANA, GODDESS OF FERTILITY. I CALL TO YOU THAT I MAY CARRY AND BEAR A CHILD WHO SHALL BE BORN OF LOVE AND CHERISHED AS A CHILD OF BLESSED LIFE. GRANT MY WISH AND HELP ME TO CONCEIVE.

Say this nine times, saying: "Thank you" at the ninth request. Visualize new life entering and filling you as you attach the nuts and cones to your garland.

4 Decorate the garland with cinnamon sticks and green ribbon, and sprinkle it with rice wine if you wish. When the garland is completed, stand up and say:

> SO MOTE IT BE, MAY DIVINE
> WILL BE DONE.

5 Beginning in the east, close your spell widdershins first and then your circle. Gather all the organic ingredients and dispose of them on the earth outside.

6 Place the garland above your nuptial bed. If it is biologically possible for you to conceive it is more likely now to happen, you must just relax and let it take place in its right time. If you suspect that you have any medical problems you must consult a medical practitioner.

GINGER AND PASSION

Gently inhaling the aroma of some fresh ginger root stimulates passion and desire in the male. Females can carry a small piece of ginger root to arouse a man's passion. Men, too, can carry a piece of it to increase their sexual magnetism. Ginger tea is a good drink for lovers to drink together to increase their sexual energy.

HOUSE BLESSING SPELL

IF YOU HAVE MOVED INTO A NEW HOUSE, AS WELL AS PERFORMING THIS SPELL YOU CAN ALSO
SWEEP EACH ROOM WITH A BIRCH BROOM. WORK CLOCKWISE AND SWEEP INTO THE CENTRE,
IMAGINING UNSEEN PSYCHIC MATTER BEING SWEPT UP AS WELL. GATHER THE SWEEPINGS
IN A PAPER CARRIER BAG AND EMPTY IT IN THE GARDEN OR BURN IT OUTSIDE.

YOU WILL NEED
- Natural sea salt
- Small bowl
- Rose geranium oil
- White candle
- Aromatherapy burner
- Spring water
- A few grains of
  organic rice
- 15 cm (6 in) square
  of golden fabric

ENVIRONMENT

 This spell should only be performed on a Sunday, just before and through midday, during a waxing (new) moon. There should be no-one else in the house.

1 Bless and consecrate yourself, using the Angel Spell. Place the salt in the bowl. Starting in the top right-hand corner of the house, sprinkle a pinch of salt in the four corners of the room, and all corners of every window and door. Proceed clockwise around the house. As you sprinkle repeat:

**I CLEANSE AND PURIFY THIS
ROOM OF ALL UNNECESSARY OR
NEGATIVE VIBRATIONS.**

2 Take the rose geranium oil and light the white candle. Working clockwise around the house, place the candle in the centre of each room. Anoint all doors and windows with a little rose geranium oil as you say:

**I CALL UPON THE ANGELS OF LIGHT AND
LOVE TO BLESS THIS HOME AND ALL WHO
ENTER HERE. MAY LOVE, HAPPINESS, AND
HARMONY PREVAIL.**

Birch is one of the purifying trees and has long been used to cleanse environments both psychically and physically. Birch twigs were traditionally used annually to beat the bounds of the parish, and are also used for broomsticks, so that as the floor of a house is brushed clean it is also purified by the power of the tree.

3 Place the candle in the centre of your living room. Add six drops of rose geranium oil to the lit aromatherapy burner filled with spring water. Sit quietly, visualizing your home filled with the qualities that you desire.

4 Let the candle burn down almost completely. Anoint the candle with rose geranium oil and sprinkle with rice as thanks to the helpful energies, then fold it into the gold fabric. Place the parcel beneath your front door mat or as close to your door as possible saying:

**THIS I PLACE SO THAT ALL WHO ENTER
HERE WILL BE BLESSED.**

5 Leave the parcel undisturbed until the time when you next perform a blessing, when it can be replaced by a new parcel.

HORSESHOES
Horsehoes are an ancient symbol of protection, and are traditionally hung on a front door. They are made from iron, a metal sacred to Mars, and therefore they ensure protection and strength for the occupants of the house. A horseshoe should be nailed firmly to the outside of the door, with the open ends upwards, preferably using iron nails.

ANGEL SPELL

THIS SPELL CAN BE PERFORMED AS ANOTHER WAY TO BLESS AND CONSECRATE YOURSELF,
OR TO HELP YOU OR THOSE YOU KNOW IN TIMES OF VULNERABILITY. YOU CAN USE THIS SPELL
WITHOUT CANDLES AND INCENSE, WHEN YOU FEEL IT IS NECESSARY, BY JUST SAYING THE INVOCATION
TO THE ANGELS. ALWAYS REMEMBER TO THANK THESE MIGHTY BEINGS OF LIGHT;
WHETHER YOU SENSE THEIR PRESENCE OR NOT, THEY WILL BE THERE.

YOU WILL NEED
◆ 9 m (29¹/₂ ft) thin
  white cord
◆ White candle
◆ Frankincense
◆ Charcoal
◆ Charcoal burner

*Take time to conjure up
your visualization of the
angels, so that you truly
"see" them in your mind.*

BLESSING YOURSELF

1 Open your cord circle and place the candle
and frankincense in the centre. Facing
south, light the candle and the burner. Add the
frankincense to the hot charcoal saying:

LORD OF LIGHT, THIS
OFFERING I MAKE.

Say the Angelic Invocation. While you say the
first line, touch your head, touching your
stomach say the second line, touching your left
shoulder say the third line, and touching your
right shoulder complete the invocation:

URIEL ABOVE ME.
MICHAEL BENEATH ME.
RAPHAEL TO MY LEFT
GABRIEL TO MY RIGHT.
BY THE POWER OF THESE
GREAT ANGELS, SURROUND
ME WITH LIGHT.

Visualize four angels in the four directions.
Bow your head and say "Thank you" to each
one. Ask them for what you feel you need. This
could be humility, an open heart, strength,
honesty or another helpful attribute for the
task at hand.

2 When your call for assistance is completed,
say "Thank you" again. Blow out the candle
and close your circle in the usual way.

BLESSING ANOTHER

1 If someone you know is in need of angelic
protection or healing, you can make an
Angel Altar. Place a white candle and
frankincense within a circle of salt, enclosed
with a recent photograph of the person.

2 Light the candle and frankincense. Say the
Angelic Invocation, touching the head and
relevant parts of the body in the photo and
saying his/her name.

*Salt is part of the crystal
kingdom and is the
blessed representation of
the earth. Use salt to
purify, consecrate and
to protect.*

3 Leave the altar for
24 hours, then
remove the circle of
salt, gathering it up so
that it can be
sprinkled on the earth
outside (or in a pot of
earth).

4 For serious situa-
tions, do the
blessing every 48
hours until you feel
your work is done.
Leave the altar for 24
hours then remove the
salt, leaving the circle
for 24 hours. Repeat
the salt circle and
invocation and remove
the salt after 24 hours.

SPELL TO FIND LOST OBJECTS

THIS IS A VISUALIZATION SPELL, IN WHICH YOU IMAGINE A LOST OBJECT BEING DRAWN BACK TO YOU. MAKE SURE THAT YOU ARE NOT DISTURBED OR YOUR ATTENTION DISTRACTED WHILE YOU ARE PERFORMING IT, OTHERWISE YOU WILL NOT BE ABLE TO FOCUS YOUR ENERGY.

YOU WILL NEED
- 20 cm (8 in) wand of hazel
- Honeysuckle oil
- Yellow cloth

PREPARATION

Cut the wand from a hazel tree, asking permission of the tree first. Cut it gently and say "Thank you". Leave a gift of a lock of your hair.

A hazel wand increases the magic of spells as well as giving magical protection during a ceremony. A forked hazel twig has long been used for water divining.

1 Draw a deosil (clockwise) circle around yourself with the hazel wand, saying:

BY THE POWERS OF HEAVEN AND EARTH I CAST THIS SACRED CIRCLE IN THE NAME OF LOVE, LIGHT, WISDOM AND TRUTH.

2 Perform the energetic breathing exercise. Anoint your temples, forehead and hands with honeysuckle oil. Sit or stand in the north, facing south and imagine that you are sitting upon a high mountain made of magnetic crystals. You can see for miles in any direction.

3 Visualize yourself opening your hands, so that the palms are facing upwards. Let us say that you have lost your keys. Say the following invocation:

SWIFT AND SURE, MY KEYS RETURN TO ME.

4 Imagine that your keys are being drawn back to you, by the strength of the magnetic mountain. Draw them back with as much willpower and concentrated thought as you can. Note any pictures that come into your mind and from which direction your keys return to your hands in the visualization.

5 To add to the spell's effectiveness, write what you have lost on a piece of paper and pin it up in your house until the object returns. If the lost object is in someone else's possession, he/she should feel compelled to return it quickly. If nothing happens, you can either try again or accept that the item is irretrievable at this time.

6 Say "Thank you" as usual to the energies that have helped you. Close your spell then move your wand widdershins from the end to the beginning of the original circle, saying:

THIS SPELL IS DONE.

Store the hazel wand wrapped in a yellow cloth in a sacred space, such as an altar or the cupboard where you keep your blessed and consecrated magical equipment.

Honeysuckle increases clairvoyant abilities and helps the mind to be receptive. It is linked to Jupiter, the planet of good luck, and so helps to bring about the desired result of finding what you are looking for.

SPELL FOR SPIRITUAL CONNECTIONS

THIS SPELL IS TO IMPROVE YOUR SPIRITUAL UNDERSTANDING, EXPAND PERCEPTION AND INCREASE CONNECTEDNESS TO THE SPIRITS OR BEINGS OF LIGHT. THE SIX-POINTED STAR IS A POWERFUL MYSTICAL SYMBOL. SITTING WITHIN IT, SURROUNDED BY VIOLET CANDLES AND AMETHYSTS, YOU WILL FEEL YOURSELF FILLED WITH SPIRITUAL LIGHT AND BE ABLE TO DRAW DOWN THE QUALITIES BESTOWED BY THE ANGELS.

YOU WILL NEED
- Lotus oil
- Rhythmic spiritual drumming music
- Natural sea salt
- 6 violet candles
- 6 amethysts
- Gold candle

Amethyst is a highly spiritual stone, linked to the crown chakra, the chakra of spirituality and the mind. It is used to increase spirituality and to aid peaceful sleep.

1 Bless all of your equipment for this spell. Facing east anoint your head, hands and feet with lotus oil. Play your spiritual drumming music.

2 Draw a six-pointed star in salt around you, made of two equal-sized triangles. The star should be large enough for you to sit in the centre.

3 Sit or stand in the centre of the star and place one of the violet candles on each of the six points, beginning with the point that is nearest to the south. As you light the first candle, say:

O ANGEL GABRIEL, LIFT MY SPIRIT TO TOUCH LEVANAH, TO DRAW DOWN HER MAGIC INTO MY HEART.

Light the candle to your right, saying:
O ANGEL RAPHAEL, LIFT MY SPIRIT TO TOUCH KOKAB THAT I MAY DRAW DOWN HIS WISDOM AND TRUTH.

Turn to the next candle and light it, saying:
O ANGEL ZAMAEL, LIFT MY SPIRIT TO TOUCH MADIM THAT I MAY DRAW DOWN COURAGE AND STRENGTH.

Turn to the next candle and light it, saying:
O ANGEL CASSIEL, LIFT MY SPIRIT TO TOUCH SHABBATHAI, THAT I MAY DRAW DOWN UNDERSTANDING AND PATIENCE.

Turn to the next candle and light it, saying:
O ANGEL SACHIEL, LIFT MY SPIRIT TO TOUCH TZEDEK THAT I MAY DRAW DOWN RIGHTEOUSNESS.

Turn to the sixth candle and light it, saying:
O ANGEL ANAEL, LIFT MY SPIRIT TO TOUCH NOGAH THAT I MAY DRAW DOWN LOVE AND BEAUTY.

THE LOTUS

The lotus symbolizes spiritual enlightenment. When linked to the crown chakra, it is known as the thousand-petalled lotus, symbolizing spiritual blossoming to the light.

4 When all the candles are lit, place an amethyst next to each one. Light the gold candle and place it in front of you inside the star, and say:

MIGHTY MICHAEL, ANGEL OF THE SUN, LIFT MY SPIRIT TO TOUCH SHEMESH THAT I MAY BE DRAWN CLOSER AND CLOSER TO THE LIGHT OF THE DIVINE. THIS I ASK OF YOU, THAT I MAY GROW EVER CLOSER TO THE TRUTH. ADONAI, LORD OF LIGHT, ADONAI, ADONAI.

5 Play the rhythmical drumming music quietly. Sit with your hands open upon your lap and let yourself be filled with the essence of spiritual light for up to 20 minutes.

6 Close your spell by picking up the amethysts then blowing out the candles, starting with the last one you lit and ending with the first.

7 Close your cord circle, saying:

MAY DIVINE WILL BE DONE.

FRIENDSHIP SPELL

PERFORM THIS SPELL WITHIN A HORSESHOE SHAPE SET INSIDE YOUR MAGICAL CORD CIRCLE.
THE COLOUR GREEN AND THE APPLE ARE BOTH SACRED TO VENUS, AND SWEET PEAS
ARE THE TRADITIONAL FLOWER OF FRIENDSHIP.

YOU WILL NEED
- 9 m (29$\frac{1}{2}$ ft) thin white cord
- 7 green candles
- Aromatherapy burner
- Sweet pea aromatherapy oil, diluted in sesame oil
- 5 seeds from a sweet organic apple
- Gold pen
- Natural paper

ENVIRONMENT
  Perform this spell on a Friday during a waxing (new) moon.

PREPARATION
Bathe, and then massage your whole body with diluted sweet pea oil.

Apples are sacred to Venus. They represent love, beauty and harmony. Share an apple with a lover to ensure a deepening bond.

1 Open the cord circle. Place the green candles in a horseshoe shape, with the open end facing north and you facing south in front of it.

2 Place the aromatherapy burner in the centre of the horseshoe shape and add seven drops of sweet pea oil. Lay the apple seeds in the centre also. Light the first candle to your left, saying:

NOGAH, NOGAH, LIGHT OF LOVE,
I HONOUR AND ILLUMINATE YOUR BEAUTY
AND CALL UPON YOU TO HELP ME TODAY.

3 Light the next candle with the lit one, then put the first candle down. Continue this way until all the candles are lit. Now light the aromatherapy burner.

4 Take the gold pen and write down your wish on the paper as follows:

BY THE POWERS OF THE FOUR
DIRECTIONS, ABOVE ME AND BELOW ME,
WITHIN ME AND WITHOUT,
I CALL FOR FAVOUR WITH ANAEL,
I CALL FOR FRIENDS OF THE SAME
HEART, THAT JOY AND CELEBRATION
SHALL PREVAIL.

5 Draw the seal of Venus, shown in the picture opposite, above your words. Pick up your wish and burn it in the flames of the last candle that you lit, visualizing as you do so that your wish is being carried to the skies.

6 Blow out the candles widdershins, saying on the last one "So mote it be". Close your circle in the usual way. Take the apple seeds to a prepared site or pot and dedicate them:

NOGAH, THESE APPLE SEEDS I PLANT TO
HONOUR YOU AND PLEASE YOU. AND AS
THEY GROW, SO IS MY LIFE BLESSED WITH
JOY OF FRIENDSHIPS NEW.

Spell for Good Luck

The power of this spell comes from the mighty oak tree, which lives for hundreds of years and is a symbol of strength. You can purchase a spell bag from a New Age shop, but making one yourself will increase the potency of the spell it contains.

You Will Need

- Small amethyst
- Turquoise crystal
- Oak leaves
- Cinquefoil oil
- Sprig of rosemary
- Spell bag

Environment

  This spell is to be performed on a Thursday during a full moon. Perform it beneath an oak tree that looks healthy and strong.

Preparation

On the Thursday a week before you weave your spell, make a spell bag and decorate it with sequin stars.

To Make a Spell Bag

Any kind of spell bag will do. Make a drawstring bag in this way. You will need: 30 cm (12 in) purple silk, 30 cm (12 in) purple and gold metallic organza, pins, needle and matching sewing thread, paper, pencil, a compass, chalk, cord, masking tape, safety pin, 1.3 m (4¼ ft) gold lace, star and moon sequins and/or beads, 2 gold tassels.

1 Pin and stitch together the two squares of material leaving a 5 cm (2 in) gap along one edge. Trim and turn through. Slip stich the gap, then top stitch 5cm (2in) from the edge. To make the drawstring, draw a 25 cm (10 in) circle on the paper and cut out. Pin this template to the purple side of the bag and draw round the edge with chalk. Stitch along the line, then stitch another circle, 2 cm (¾ in) further in for the drawstring channel. Fold the bag in half widthways to mark the centre. Cut a small hole through the organza channel at each end of the centre fold. Overstitch the edges to make eyelets.

2 Cut the cord in half and bind the raw ends with masking tape. Fasten a safety pin to the end of one piece and, starting and finishing at one of the eyelets, thread it through the channel. Stitch the two ends together. Thread the other piece in the same way through the other hole.

3 Decorate the bag: slip stitch the gold lace around the outside edge of the bag, sew the sequins on the bag, and attach the tassels.

The Spell

1 Greet your oak tree and tell it your intentions. Place an offering of a small amethyst at its base. Walking deosil in a circle, repeat four times:

O Sachiel, it is I (name). I ask you to hear my call. Light my path, guide my actions, words and deeds and those of all I am yet to meet, that by the power of your might, all will be fortunate to my sight.
Good fortune growing, growing,
growing,
growing.

The oak is a guardian tree, with great strength and courage. Sacred to the Druids, it is the tree of Jupiter and a fortunate tree to befriend.

2 Anoint the turquoise crystal and leaves with cinquefoil oil, while visualizing yourself surrounded by the arms of a mighty oak.

3 Place the crystal, the sprig of rosemary and the oak leaves in your spell bag. Hold it up to the oak tree and say:

> HEART OF OAK, YOU ARE MY
> HEART AND WITH HONOUR I SHALL
> CARRY YOU BY MY SIDE.
> THANK YOU.

4 Carry your spell with you at all times when you seek good fortune, and store it carefully when not in use.

Spell for the Earth

Choose a place where mankind is using, or abusing, the earth's resources, for example a polluted river or a quarry. Stand as near as possible without arousing curiosity to perform this spell of atonement. The spell can be performed at any time.

You Will Need
- Moss agate crystal
- White rose

Moss agate helps us to communicate with the elemental kindgom, especially when calling for stability on the earth. It is an important stone when performing healing ceremonies for our planet.

1 Hold the moss agate crystal in your right hand and the rose in your left, and say the following prayer of atonement:

Spirits of this place, I come
in peace but with a heavy heart.
I wish to say how sorry
I am for what my brothers and
sisters are doing to you in their
ignorance. I come to make an
offering to show you that I am
sorry for taking
from you without respect.
I ask your forgiveness.
I ask you to help humanity to see
how precious all life is.
I make this offering
(Lay down your moss agate)
To you.

2 Transfer the rose to your right hand. Hold it to your heart, say:

Creator, guide us all in the ways of
peace, love, wisdom and truth. I call
you here to (name the place) to bring
the Divine to this area, to bless it
with your healing love.
May (name the place) now be
sacred again.

3 Lay down the white rose on the earth. Visualize the whole area filling with white light, embracing it with illumination.

4 If you wish, end the spell with a Native American saying "Mitake Oyassin" (we are all related), or your own personal saying.

HEALING SPELL

BEFORE YOU PERFORM THIS SPELL, FIND A SUITABLE TREE TO BURY IT UNDER – ASH, BIRCH, JUNIPER, ORANGE AND CEDAR TREES ALL HAVE HEALING POWERS. INVOKE THE POWERS OF FRESH GREEN LIME FRUIT, TO HELP RESTORE HEALTH TO YOURSELF OR TO ANOTHER PERSON.

YOU WILL NEED
- 9 m (29½ ft) thin white cord
- Gold candle
- Gold pen
- 15 cm (6 in) square of natural paper
- Knife
- Lime
- Gold thread
- 15 cm (6 in) square of orange cloth

ENVIRONMENT
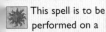 This spell is to be performed on a Sunday.

3 Cut the lime lengthways into two. Fold the paper three times and place between the two lime halves. Bind the lime halves together with gold thread, saying the following invocation:

POWERS OF LIME,
HEALTH IS MINE/THINE.
CLEANSE THE BODY,
CLEANSE
THE MIND.
SPIRIT PURE, FILL
MY (or person's)
BEING WITH HEALTH, WITH
HEALTH,
WITH HEALTH.

4 Place the bound lime in the orange cloth and bind the cloth with gold thread. Close the circle in the usual way.

1 Open the circle and honour the four directions. Light the candle, saying:

ANGEL OCH, I LIGHT THIS FLAME TO HONOUR YOUR PRESENCE AND ASK YOU TO HEAR THIS PRAYER.

2 Write your or another person's name with the gold pen on the paper, at the same time visualizing health and wellbeing surrounding you or them.

5 Bury the parcel in the earth, under an ash, birch, juniper, orange or cedar tree. Ask the tree to help you return to good health and thank the tree.

Spell to Stop Gossip

Bury the source of the malicious gossip beneath a holly tree, and ask the tree to protect your good name. The snapdragon is a flower children play with, imagining it can speak as its petals are opened and closed. There is great wisdom in this, as snapdragon is a traditional cure for jaw and throat problems.

You Will Need
- 9 m (29¹/₂ ft) thin white cord
- Blessed red candle
- Red pen
- A very small square of natural paper
- Snapdragon (*Antirrhinum*) flower
- Thorn
- Red ribbon

Environment

This spell should be performed on a Tuesday, during a waning moon.

Preparation

Find a holly tree to bury your spell under, you might want to perform your spell next to it too.

1 Open your cord circle. Light the red candle, face south and sit down.

2 Write in red pen on the paper square the name of the person or organization that is gossiping about you. If you do not know the name, write "whoever is".

3 Carefully take one of the larger flowers from the stem of the snapdragon and gently open it up. Fold the piece of paper or roll into a tiny scroll and place it inside the flower, repeating five times:

SPEAK ONLY GOODNESS, THINK ONLY KIND. LOOK TO YOUR OWN FAULTS AND NOT TO MINE.

Holly is sacred to Mars. Use it to call for protection or to banish conflicts.

4 Keep the scroll of paper in place by sealing the flower head with the thorn, as you do this say:

FLOWER SEAL, FLOWER HEAL LIPS THAT SPEAK NOT FROM THE HEART.

5 Take your spell to a holly tree, tell it of your intentions to bury it there and ask its protection over your good name.

6 Bury the snapdragon flower head under the holly tree. Say "Thank you" by tying a small red ribbon to a branch.

7 Leave, visualizing as you walk away, that you are leaving the malicious gossip behind you. Do not look back.

SPELL FOR REMOVING CONFLICT

THIS SPELL WILL HELP REMOVE CONFLICT IN A RELATIONSHIP. IT WILL WORK BEST IF BOTH PEOPLE IN THE RELATIONSHIP PERFORM IT TOGETHER. IF ONLY ONE OF YOU WISHES TO DO IT, WRITE DOWN WHAT YOU WISH TO LET GO OF, DON'T CONCERN YOURSELF WITH YOUR PARTNER'S RETICENCE AND WORK INSTEAD TO HEAL YOUR OWN DIFFICULTIES.

YOU WILL NEED
- 5.5 m (18 ft) white cord
- A small round table or stool
- 5 red candles
- Charcoal
- Heatproof container
- Coriander seeds
- Red pen
- Two pieces of natural paper

ENVIRONMENT

  This spell should be performed on a Tuesday during a waning moon.

1 Open your cord circle. Place the round table or stool in the centre of the circle and on it position the red candles, also in a circle, and light them, remembering which candle is the last to be lit.

2 Light the charcoal in the heatproof container. When it is hot, face west and sprinkle on the coriander seeds, saying:

O ANGEL ZAMAEL, WE CALL UPON YOU TO HELP US TODAY/ TONIGHT, AND DEDICATE THIS OFFERING TO YOU.

TO MAKE A WISH
Write your names together on natural paper, stating a positive wish you both want. Place it in the centre of an organic apple, cut in half. Seal with green candle wax and bury it near to the house in a prepared spot. If the apple seeds grow, tend them carefully because they represent new growth in your relationship.

3 Breathe in the aroma of the burning seeds. Each person should then use the red pen to write on their piece of paper the emotion you want to let go of – jealousy, anger, hurt etc.

4 Add your negative feelings to the piece of paper. Then walk widdershins around the table five times, visualizing your emotion and the way you express it.

5 After you have circled the table for the fifth time, each of you should burn your own piece of paper in the flame of the last candle that was lit.

SPELL TO SELL YOUR HOUSE

BURNING FRANKINCENSE WILL CLEANSE YOUR HOME AND PURIFY IT OF OLD VIBRATIONS, MAKING IT READY FOR THE NEXT KEEPER. A VASE OF FLOWERS PLACED IN A ROOM ON THE APPROPRIATE DAY OF THE WEEK CAN MAGICALLY ENHANCE YOUR WISHES.

YOU WILL NEED

- Frankincense
- Yellow flowers
- Lavender incense
- Front door key
- Yellow ribbon

ENVIRONMENT

This spell is to be performed on a Wednesday, during a waxing (new) moon.

1 Clean and tidy your house thoroughly, then burn frankincense in all the rooms, saying:

NOW IS TIME FOR ME/US TO LEAVE. WITH THANKS I/WE CLEANSE YOU.

2 Face west, the direction for letting go. As you say the invocation turn from west to east moving deosil:

I/WE LET GO OF THIS PLACE,
SO THAT A NEW BEGINNING
MAY ARISE.

3 Place yellow flowers in the living room and burn lavender incense. Tell the house spirit that you wish to depart and need the next keepers to come and take over from you.

THE FLOWERS OF THE WEEK

SATURDAY	EVERGREENS, CYPRESS
SUNDAY	ORANGE FLOWERS
MONDAY	WHITE FLOWERS, RIVER PLANTS
TUESDAY	RED FLOWERS
WEDNESDAY	YELLOW FLOWERS
THURSDAY	VIOLET FLOWERS, PURPLE FLOWERS
FRIDAY	PINK FLOWERS, ROSES

4 Hang a front door key from a yellow ribbon in an east-facing window where it can blow in the wind (but not be available for burglars!). Call upon the East Wind to help you move on to new surroundings. As you hang up the key, say:

THIS PROPERTY SELLS,
THIS PROPERTY SELLS,
HERE HANGS THE KEY TO GUIDE
THE NEXT KEEPER HERE.

SPELL TABLES

These tables can be used to help
you develop your own spellweaving skills.
By referring to the lunar calendar or
planetary tables, you can begin to build a
picture of the best times and phases to weave
your magic. You will also need an
astrological almanac or
diary to refer to.

LUNAR CALENDAR

The moon travels through the 12 signs of the zodiac approximately every 28 days, passing through her own four phases during this period. The waxing moon in a sign helps new beginnings, the full moon helps fruitfulness, fertility and increase, the waning moon helps falling away and removing. It is advisable not to weave magic during the deep winter months or during the dark phases of the moon but to reflect, prepare and meditate instead.

♑	CAPRICORN	MATERIAL MATTERS AND CONCERNS, OBSTACLES
♒	AQUARIUS	HEALING, HIGHER THOUGHT, MENTAL HEALTH
♓	PISCES	PSYCHIC WORK, CREATIVE IDEAS
♈	ARIES	BUSINESS, SUCCESS, INNOVATION, LEADERSHIP
♉	TAURUS	MATERIAL MATTERS, NOURISHMENT, PHYSICAL HEALTH
♊	GEMINI	COMMUNICATION, TRAVEL, LEARNING
♋	CANCER	FAMILY, FRIENDS, EMOTIONAL HEALTH, THE HOME
♌	LEO	SUCCESS, WEALTH, RECOGNITION, GENERAL HEALTH
♍	VIRGO	HARVEST, ABUNDANCE, FRUITFULNESS
♎	LIBRA	BALANCE, HARMONY, RELATIONSHIPS
♏	SCORPIO	SEXUALITY, OCCULT, ANCESTORS, SPIRITUAL UNDERSTANDING, INSIGHT
♐	SAGITTARIUS	TRAVEL, TRANSCENDENCE, WISDOM

PLANETARY TABLE

This table gives guidelines on which day of the week is best for weaving certain spells, and lists the propitious elements associated with that planet.

SATURDAY

SATURN
Spellweave on this day to clear obstacles and restrictions.

MINERALS	JET, OBSIDIAN, LEAD
COLOUR	INDIGO/BLACK
NUMBER	3
ANGEL	CASSIEL
GODDESS	KALI
TREES	ALDER, BEECH, HOLLY, ELM, YEW
PLANTS	IVY, EVERGREENS
HERB	ASAFOETIDA
AROMA	CYPRESS

Asafoetida and jet

SUNDAY

THE SUN

Spellweave on this day to attract health, and success and prosperity.

MINERALS	TOPAZ, AMBER, GOLD
COLOUR	GOLD/ ORANGE
NUMBER	6
ANGEL	MICHAEL
GOD	RA-HARACHTE
TREES	ACACIA, BAY, BIRCH, CEDAR, WALNUT, LIME, ORANGE, ROWAN, JUNIPER
PLANTS	MISTLETOE, MARIGOLD, BAY LAUREL, BENZOIN GUM, ANGELICA
HERB	CINNAMON, BAY LEAVES
AROMA	FRANKINCENSE

MONDAY

THE MOON

Spellweave on this day to increase intuition, perceptions, fertility and all female issues.

MINERALS	PEARL, MOONSTONE, SILVER
COLOUR	SILVER/BLUE
NUMBER	9
ANGEL	GABRIEL
GODDESS	SELENE
TREES	ASPEN, WILLOW, LEMON, EUCALYPTUS
PLANTS	JASMINE, POPPY, WHITE LILY SEA PLANTS, RIVER PLANTS
HERB	SANDALWOOD
AROMA	JASMINE

Lemon

TUESDAY

MARS

Spellweave on this day to improve strength, power and authority and to banish conflicts.

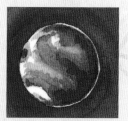

MINERALS	HEMATITE, RUBY, IRON
COLOUR	RED
NUMBER	5
ANGEL	ZAMAEL
GODDESS	ANATH
TREES	LARCH, HAWTHORN, DOGWOOD
PLANTS	ANEMONE, TOBACCO
HERB	CORIANDER, GARLIC, PEPPER
AROMA	PINE

Garlic

WEDNESDAY

MERCURY
Spellweave on this day for all forms of communication, including writing, teaching, speaking, learning, studying, and travel.

MINERALS	AGATE, CARNELIAN, QUICKSILVER
COLOUR	YELLOW
NUMBER	8
ANGEL	RAPHAEL
GODDESS	ATHENA
TREES	ASH, HAZEL
PLANTS	IMPATIENS
HERB	CARAWAY, LAVENDER, MARJORAM, DILL
AROMA	LAVENDER

Lavender and agates

THURSDAY

JUPITER
Spellweave on this day for employment, luck, travel, money, justice and wealth.

MINERALS	AMETHYST, AQUAMARINE, TIN
COLOUR	VIOLET/ PURPLE
NUMBER	4
ANGEL	SACHIEL
GODDESS	JUNO
TREES	ALMOND, HORSE CHESTNUT, OAK
PLANTS	AVENS, HONEYSUCKLE
HERB	CINQUEFOIL, NUTMEG, SAGE, ANISE, CLOVES
AROMA	HONEYSUCKLE

nutmeg

FRIDAY

VENUS
Spellweave on this day for love, friendship, marriage, beauty and harmony and creativity.

MINERALS	EMERALD, JADE, COPPER
COLOUR	GREEN
NUMBER	7
ANGEL	ANAEL
GODDESS	APHRODITE
TREES	APPLE, FIG, MAGNOLIA, PEAR, ELDER, DAMSON,
PLANTS	HEATHER, HYACINTH, ROSE, LOVE-IN-A-MIST, IRIS, PERIWINKLE, VIOLET
HERB	VERVAIN, MYRTLE, YARROW
AROMA	ROSE

Spells and Nature

The high magician works very closely with nature, communing with planets and stars, trees, plants, fairies, devas, angels, animals, stones, crystals and the elements of earth, air, fire and water. Following the circle of life and the wheel of the year, there are many ways to weave a magical nature spell.

Birds and Their Meanings

Any feathers that you find can be used in spellweaving. The birds themselves have particular messages and meanings, and you can use the appropriate feathers for magical spells.

Blackbird	Gatekeeper
Crow	Change
Duck	Love and Harmony
Eagle	Clarity
Hawk	Foresight
Magpie	Relationships
Owl	Wisdom
Pigeon	Messages
Robin	Protection
Swan	Purity
Woodpecker	Magic and Prophecy
Wren	Protection

Stones and Their Meanings

Stones, crystals and gems are used a great deal in natural magic. Here are a few and their meanings to me. Work with stones that have particular meaning for you.

Agate	For inspiration from the spiritual realms
Amethyst	Mental and spiritual balance
Aquamarine	To increase psychic powers
Citrine	The prosperity stone
Celestite	To link with angels
Flint	Psychic protection
Fossil	To link with earth wisdom
Moss Agate	Earth healing
Seashell	Fertility
Smoky Quartz	Absorbs negative vibrations, grounds and stabilizes
Turquoise	Healing and protection
Vanadinite	Mental focus, life direction

TREES AND THEIR MEANINGS

Trees and plants have particular qualities and abilities. This table will help you to choose an appropriate tree according to the spell you are weaving.

HEALING SPELLS	ASH, ASPEN, ELDER, EUCALYPTUS
SPIRITUAL SPELLS	ALDER, BAMBOO, PINE, WITCH HAZEL, YEW
PURIFICATION SPELLS	BAY, BIRCH, BROOM, CEDAR, TAMARISK, WILLOW
PROTECTION SPELLS	ASH, CYPRESS, HOLLY, LARCH, MULBERRY, ROWAN, OAK
FERTILITY SPELLS	BANANA, BIRCH, FIG, HAZELNUT, OAK, PINE (CONES), WALNUT, WILLOW
INCREASE THE MAGIC OF SPELLS	APPLE, ASH, HAZEL, ROWAN, WILLOW, WITCH HAZEL
LOVE SPELLS	APPLE, APRICOT, POMEGRANATE, NUT, WILLOW
PROSPERITY SPELLS	ALMOND, HORSE CHESTNUT

GLOSSARY

ANGELS:
ANAEL Angel of the planet Venus
CASSIEL Angel of the planet Saturn
GABRIEL Angel of the moon
MICHAEL Angel of the sun, the leading angel
OCH Healing spirit of the sun
RAPHAEL Angel of the planet Mercury
SACHIEL Angel of the planet Jupiter
URIEL Angel of the north and Earth
ZAMAEL Angel of the planet Mars

ADONI Hebrew name meaning lord of light.

BELTANE Celtic May Day fertility festival to mark the beginning of summer.

CHAKRA Sanskrit word for "wheel", names the body's centres of energy.

CROWN CHAKRA Energy centre found at the top of the head.

DEOSIL To move in a clockwise direction.

DEVAS A name for beings of the light.

DIANA Goddess of fertility, linked to the full moon.

EQUINOXES Two fixed points of the year, spring and autumn

ESBATS Times of lunar celebration.

HARA The place of inner knowing located in the abdomen.

IMBOLC Celtic festival marking spring.

KOKAB Hebrew name for the planet Mercury.

LAMMAS Celtic festival of the harvest.

LEVANAH Hebrew name for the moon.

MADIM Hebrew name for the planet Mars.

MOTE Old English word meaning "shall".

NOGAH Hebrew name for the planet Venus.

SAMHAINE Celtic festival, also known as Hallowe'en.

SHABBATHAI Hebrew name for the planet Saturn.

SHEMESH Hebrew name for the sun.

SIGIL A pictorial depiction of a name.

SMUDGING Cleansing, using the smoke of burning herbs.

SOLSTICES Two fixed points of the year, marking midwinter and midsummer.

TZEDEK Hebrew name for the planet Jupiter.

WANING The moon's decrease in influence.

WAXING The moon's increase in influence.

WIDDERSHINS To move anti-clockwise (counter-clockwise).

INDEX

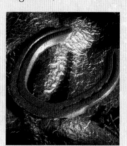

SUPPLIERS

UK
Sally Morningstar
www.sallymorningstar.com
Spellweaving, shamanism, spiritual courses and consultations.

The Blissful Pixie
www.theblissfulpixie.wix.com/emporium
Supplier of magical and spiritual items

G Baldwin & Co.
www.baldwins.co.uk
High-grade herbs, tinctures and oils.

Pagan Federation
www.paganfed.org
Information on suppliers of magical equipment.

UNITED STATES
Branwen's Cauldron of Light
www.branwenscauldron.com
Essential oils, candles and gemstones and other magical equipment

Strange Brew
www.the cauldron.com
Essential oils, herbs and incense.